TOM PATTY'S
MARKETING *Without* MONEY WORKBOOK

SARAI KOO, PH.D.

© Sarai Koo, Ph.D. All rights reserved. Do not copy or distribute without permission.

Tom Patty's MARKETING WITHOUT MONEY

Written by Tom Patty and Donna Jost

Tom Patty's MARKETING WITHOUT MONEY WORKBOOK

Written by Sarai Koo, Ph.D.

Tom Patty granted Dr. Sarai Koo permission to create a marketing workbook based on his book Tom's Patty Marketing Without Money

"Marketing is dependent on ideas." – Tom Patty

Sarai Koo, Ph.D.
Project SPICES
SPICES Publications

Copyright © 2021 Sarai Koo

All rights reserved. No part of this publication, which includes concepts and ideas may be reproduced, distributed, stored in a retrieval system, translated in another language, or transmitted in any form or by any means, including photocopying, recording, or other electronic or mechanical methods, without the prior written permission of the Author, except in the case of brief quotations embodied in critical reviews and certain other noncommercial uses permitted by copyright law. For permission requests, email the author at info@projectspices.com.

Disclaimer: This program and publication contain the opinions and concepts of its author. The program is the proprietary property of Dr. Sarai Koo. Dr. Koo owns the intellectual property of the Program, which include all rights, title, and interest in and to the Program. This program cannot be administered, distributed, and sold without prior training from Dr. Koo.

ISBN 978-0-9907750-4-1
EBook 978-0-9907750-5-8

Contents

Workbook Overview 7
   Tom Patty's Brief Biography 7
   How I Met Tom 7

Preface 9

Chapter 1: Marketing is to Business What Sex is to People 13

Part One: What? 15

Chapter 2. What Does "Marketing Without Money" Really Mean? 15

Chapter 3. What Marketing "Is" and "Is Not" 17
      Marketing Requires Ability 19
      Attraction Defined 20
      Packaging 21
      Product or Service (Character/Personality) 21
      Distribution (How Accessible Am I?) 22
      Value (Benefits / Cost) 22
      Promotion (Be Better Known) 23

Chapter 4. What You Need to Know About Social Media 25

Chapter 5. Back to Basics: Are They a Market for Your Goods or Services? 27

Part II: How? 29

Chapter 6. Marketing Leverage: How Other Companies Used "The Big 5" to Grow Their Businesses 29
      Strategy 1. Solve More Consumer Needs or Wants 29
      Strategy 2. Be More Attractive (Packaging) 31
      Strategy 3. Be More Convenient 32
      Strategy 4. Create a Better Value (Price) 33
      Strategy 5. Be Better Known (Promotion) 34

Chapter 7. How to Select the Right Target Audience 37
      How to Define Your Target Audience 37
      Sometimes Your Clients Choose You 37

Chapter 8. How to Use Your Best Customers to Grow Your Business 39

Chapter 9. How to Promote One Benefit 41
      Consumer's Point of View 41

What Do You Stand for? 43

Chapter 10. How to Improve Your Value Equation 47

Chapter 11. How to Understand and Use the Purchase Funnel.. 49

What is the Purchase Funnel? 49

How Will I Move My Customers Down the Purchase Funnel?................................... 50

Chapter 12. How to Use the Right Strategy to Grow Your Business............................. 51

Product-Oriented Business..52

Service-Oriented Business...52

Typical 4 Stage Process to Acquire New Customers 53

Chapter 13. The Importance of You 55

Have the End in Mind..55

Chapter 14. Conclusion 57

Biography 59

Workbook Overview

Tom Patty's Brief Biography

Tom Patty has extensive experience in marketing and advertising. He was the former president, Worldwide Account Director of the Los Angeles office at TBWA/Chiat/Day Advertising Agency. He retired in 1998 at the age of 53. His clientele included Apple, Pizza Hut, Nike, Nissan, Infiniti, and Yamaha motorcycles to name a few.

How I Met Tom

As an entrepreneur without millions of dollars to launch my business ideas, I signed up for various counseling, seminars and workshops to help my businesses get launched. One of the programs that I signed up for was at SCORE, "a nonprofit association dedicated to helping small businesses get off the ground, grow and achieve their goals through education and mentorship" in Orange County, California. In 2015, I attended a workshop presented by Tom Patty and John Pietro (Senior Marketing Executive for corporations like Denny's and Wendy's. He worked on the famous "Where's The Beef" Campaign).

During the seminar there was a contest. The winner of the contest would receive FREE one-on-one sessions with both Tom and John. I never knew I had a competitive spirit until they mentioned the winning prize. I was desperate to receive the support and guidance from them. I won!

I met John and Tom at a famous coffee shop chain. My relationship with John continued while Tom desired to go out into the sea on his boat.

After reading Tom's book, I asked him if it would be possible to create a companion workbook. Since I do not have marketing skills, I used his book to help me with my mine. I extracted questions from his book chapters to help me organize my thoughts in a more coherent and useful manner. I have taken these questions turned it into a workbook for others to use.

Tom granted me permission to publish the workbook. Although it has taken me many years to finish the supplemental workbook and publish it, I hope this guide will be useful to people who read his book.

Helpful Hint: Use this workbook while you read Tom Patty's book *Marketing Without Money*. Given Tom's extensive background in marketing and advertising, perhaps using his methodology will help you become a successful entrepreneur. Some of the questions seem redundant. These somewhat repetitive questions may help you refine/narrow your thoughts.

Please note that I am not a marketing guru. I, too, am applying Tom Patty's principles.

Preface

Tom Patty once said the following: *If you want to grow your business, you need to satisfy more customers' needs.*

- Turn good ideas into good products/services
- Serve people's needs
- Make it easier for customers to gain access to your products and services
- Improve your packaging to make your products/services attractive– everything people see (website, invoice, office, business card, etc.)

Before you begin launching your business, products and services, Tom Patty agrees with Simon Sinek's idea that "people don't buy what you do; they buy why you do it."[1]

Therefore, before you begin, answer these questions:

1. What is my intended purpose in creating this business/product/service?
   _____
   _____
   _____
   _____

2. What is my *why*?
   _____
   _____
   _____
   _____

3. Who am I?
   _____
   _____
   _____
   _____

---

[1] Simon Sinek, *Start with Why: How Great Leaders Inspire Everyone to Take Action* (2011, p. 41)

4. What am I most passionate about?
_____
_____
_____
_____

5. What do I want out of my business?
_____
_____
_____
_____

6. Why am I in business?
_____
_____
_____
_____

7. What is my purpose in life?
_____
_____
_____
_____

8. How does my purpose align to my business goals?
_____
_____
_____
_____

9. Where am I currently weak in (personal)?
_____
_____
_____
_____

10. Where am I currently weak in (business)?

_____
_____
_____
_____

11. Where am I strong/good at (personal)?

_____
_____
_____
_____

12. Where am I strong/good at (business)?

_____
_____
_____
_____

Chapter 1: Marketing is to Business What Sex is to People

"Marketing . . . is about fulfilling needs and wants. A business that figures out how to satisfy more customers will be more successful than those that don't pay attention to consumers' needs." – Tom Patty[2] (p. 4)

1. In what way will my products and services satisfy my paying customers?

___

2. How have I been marketing my product and services? In what way have my marketing strategies been effective or efficient? Let's be honest, is there room for growth?

___

3. What are my marketing pain points?

___

---

[2] Quotes taken from *Tom Patty's Marketing Without Money* (2013)

Part One: What?

Chapter 2. What Does "Marketing Without Money" Really Mean?

"Sometimes in marketing it's much easier to create a new brand than to get consumers to alter the current positioning images they have in their heads."
- Tom Patty (p. 12)

1. How can I make my products and services easier and convenient for my paying customers? (Pizza Hut story)

   _____
   _____
   _____
   _____
   _____

2. Was my marketing idea bad or was the specific execution bad? (Apple Store story)

   _____
   _____
   _____
   _____
   _____

3. What is another marketing approach/concept/idea that will help me successfully execute my products and services? Think differently. (Southwest Airlines and Nissan Altima stories)

   _____
   _____
   _____
   _____
   _____

4. Sometimes it may be easier to create a new brand than to alter the brand to fit what the customer understands. How can I create a new brand for my product or service? (Lexus/Infiniti story)

_____
_____
_____
_____
_____

5. List multiple ways to market my product or service. (Wolfgang Puck Food Company story)

_____
_____
_____
_____
_____

6. Marketing content. Are there any areas I could adjust the content to attract new customers? What portions of my content would I change? What would my new message be? (write/draw)

_____
_____
_____
_____
_____
_____
_____

Chapter 3. What Marketing "Is" and "Is Not"

"Marketing is everything you can do to attract and retain more good customers [and more]." – Tom Patty (p. 21)

1. What products and services will satisfy the needs of my customers?

   _____
   _____
   _____
   _____
   _____

2. How am I packaging my products and services? How does it look, feel, etc.? Ask someone to comment on my product and service. How does it look to that person?

   _____
   _____
   _____
   _____
   _____

3. How do I distribute my products and services? Marketing is about convenience. How is it convenient for my customers?

   _____
   _____
   _____
   _____
   _____

4. How am I pricing my products and services? What is my pricing structure? How do I know if the price I offer will create value for my customers?

_____
_____
_____
_____
_____

5. How do I position my product compared to my competition? What is my promotional strategy?

Competitor's Product	My Product

_____
_____
_____

6. Marketing is about curating the right message to the right person. How do I know if I am sending the right message? Are there any messages I need to adjust?

_____
_____
_____
_____

Marketing Requires Ability

1. A good marketer should have the ability to put someone else's needs in front of his/her/their own. What do my customer's think about my product/service?

_____
_____
_____
_____

2. A good marketer is able to figure out what people want or need. Why would my prospective customers want or need my product or service?

_____
_____
_____
_____

3. A good marketer understands the difference between rational and emotional needs. Think of a product I sell. Determine the difference between rational and emotional need.

Rational Need	Emotional Need
Ex. You no longer have it.	Ex. It makes me feel.

Attraction Defined

> *"The essence of marketing is about creating attraction."* – Tom Patty (p. 25)

1. Let's take a look at my product or service. What type of customers would be drawn to my products/service? What could be done to improve my product's appeal?

_____
_____
_____
_____

2. How many people are aware of my product/service/me?

_____
_____
_____
_____

5 Ways to Increase Desirability

Packaging (Everything people see)

Product or Service (Character/Personality)

Distribution (How accessible am I?)

Value (Benefits vs. cost or baggage)

Promotion (Be better known)

Packaging

1. Who is a person or company I admire? What about this person or company makes him/her/them attractive to me?

_____
_____
_____
_____

2. Look within. How can I repackage yourself? (visually, voice, communication, style, etc.)

_____
_____
_____
_____

Product or Service (Character/Personality)

1. What products or service attract me into buying them? What about it makes it attractive?

_____
_____
_____
_____

2. In what ways can I make my product/service more attractive?

_____
_____
_____
_____

Distribution (How Accessible Am I?)

1. What products/services make it easier for me when I purchase them? What mechanisms/approach do they use? (e.g., Amazon, Zappos)

_____
_____
_____
_____

2. How do I distribute my product/service? How can I make it easier for my customers to purchase my product/service?

_____
_____
_____
_____

Value (Benefits / Cost)

1. What is my products/services value? Value equals benefits divided by cost.

_____
_____
_____
_____

2. How do I know my products are valuable—worth it?

_____
_____
_____
_____

Promotion (Be Better Known)

1. How many people in my target audience know about my product/service?

   _____
   _____
   _____
   _____

2. How many people would consider purchasing my product/service over another competitor's product/service?

   _____
   _____
   _____
   _____

3. How many people would love my product/service? Why? What's so unique/special about my product/service?

   _____
   _____
   _____
   _____

4. Overall, what are some ways to increase my business applying the five approaches?

   _____
   _____
   _____
   _____
   _____
   _____
   _____
   _____

Chapter 4. What You Need to Know About Social Media

"Facebook friends aren't there to buy; they're there to socialize." - Tom Patty (p. 39)

1. What types of social media am I using? What are my handles? Which social media accounts help me sell my products/service? (Circle the accounts)

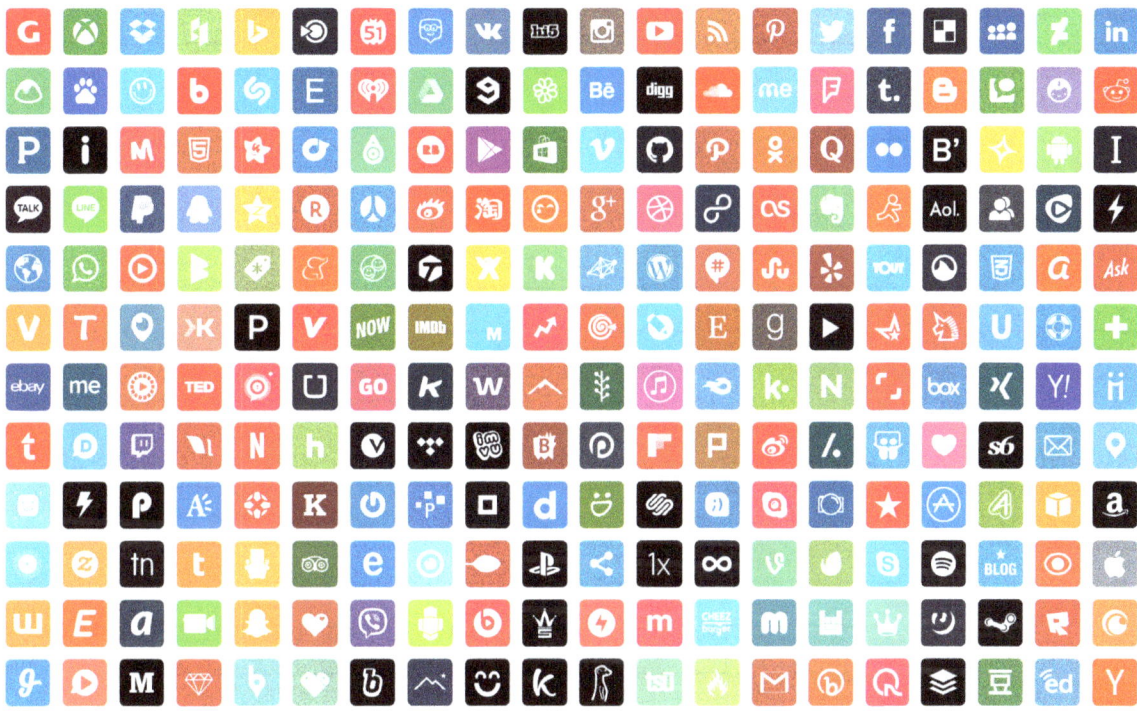

Place additional accounts and handles here:

2. Which social media accounts have brought me more paying clients?
   _____
   _____
   _____

3. Which social media accounts have been unsuccessful when I tried to sell my products/services?
   _____
   _____
   _____

4. What are some alternative ways to increase my business using social media?
   _____
   _____
   _____
   _____

5. What are alternative ways to increase my business without using social media?
   _____
   _____
   _____
   _____

Chapter 5. Back to Basics: Are They a Market for Your Goods or Services?

"It's about wanting something and being able to pay for it." – Tom Patty (p. 47)

1. What is my product or service? What does my product/service/company do for my customers? How will it improve their lives?

   _____
   _____
   _____
   _____

2. Who will buy my product or service?

   _____
   _____

3. What evidence is there the market exists for my product/service? How do I know there is a demand for my product/service?

   _____
   _____
   _____
   _____

4. Is there a demand for my product/service? How big is the total annual dollar revenue?

   _____
   _____

5. In my targeted market segment, which segments of the market are growing and which are declining?

   _____
   _____
   _____

6. Who are my competitors? Why are they my competitors?

_____
_____
_____
_____
_____

7. Why will customers buy my product/service versus my competition?

_____
_____
_____
_____
_____
_____
_____
_____

Part II: How?

Chapter 6. Marketing Leverage: How Other Companies Used "The Big 5" to Grow Their Businesses

*". . . make sure the new products or services are aligned
with the core essence of your brand."*
– Tom Patty (p. 61)

The Big 5 Strategies for Success

1. Solve more consumer needs or wants
2. Be more attractive
3. Be more convenient
4. Be a better value
5. Be better known

The Big 5	How can I implement This Strategy in My Business?
Solve more customer needs/wants	
Be more attractive	
Be more convenient	
Create a better value	
Be better known	

Strategy 1. Solve More Consumer Needs or Wants

1. How is my product/service aligned with the essence of my brand?

_____
_____
_____
_____
_____

2. What is the customer *really* buying?

What I Am Selling	Customer Is Buying
Mercedes Benz Automobiles	Distinctive, Stylish Transportation
Gym Membership	Better Physical Shape/Fitness

Found on Page 77

3. What new products or services can I provide to my customers to make them seem more valuable to them and ultimately more loyal to my business?

_____
_____
_____
_____
_____

4. What products or services am I currently selling?

_____
_____
_____

5. What needs do these products or services currently satisfy?

_____
_____
_____
_____

6. What new needs can I serve?

_____
_____
_____
_____

7. What other customer problems could I solve?

_____
_____
_____

Strategy 2. Be More Attractive (Packaging)

1. Look at a product or service I admire. How did they package this product/service? What does it feel, look, etc.? Why do I really like this product/service? Why am I drawn to it?

_____
_____
_____
_____
_____

2. How can I have my product be more attractive to someone else? (packaging)

_____
_____
_____
_____
_____

3. What can I do to make everything that people see about my business (from stationary to storefront to website) more interesting, more attractive, or more functional for my customers?

_____
_____
_____
_____

4. How can my website be improved? --- be more user-friendly? What do I want people to see, do, think when they come to my site?

_____
_____
_____
_____
_____

Strategy 3. Be More Convenient

1. How and where can customers currently buy my products or services?

_____
_____
_____
_____
_____

2. How can I make my products or services more convenient and accessible for my customers? (e.g. longer hours, more days of the week, more locations, free shipping, etc.)

_____
_____
_____
_____
_____

3. Ask people to review my product or service. How come the people do not like my product, service, delivery, attractiveness, etc.? What will I do with these reviews?

_____
_____
_____
_____

Strategy 4. Create a Better Value (Price)

1. Value is about quantifying what is deemed important to people. What products or services do I place value on? What types of products and services (or name brands) am I willing to pay more for?

   _____
   _____
   _____
   _____
   _____

2. What's the current value of my program or service? (price) Value = Benefits/Cost

   _____
   _____
   _____
   _____
   _____

3. How would I position my product against a competitor's product or service? How can I increase my perceived quality of service?

   _____
   _____
   _____
   _____
   _____

4. In what ways can I improve my product's quality and performance and/or level of service?

   _____
   _____
   _____
   _____

5. How can my company (product/service) be better than my competitors in one or two dimensions of:

Quality (performance, safer, cleaner more dependable)
_____
_____

Service (faster, more convenient, easy to use, nicer, friendlier, more honest, trustworthy)?
_____
_____

Strategy 5. Be Better Known (Promotion)

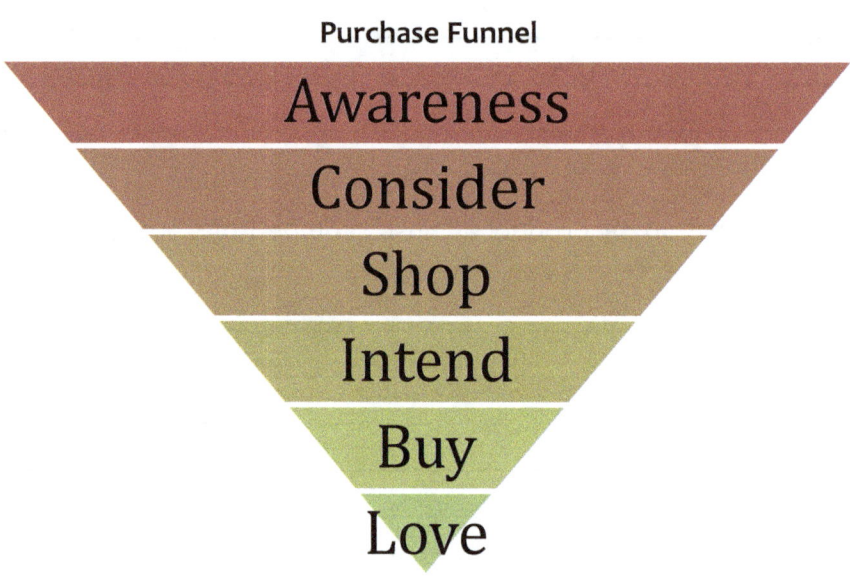

1. How do I generate awareness for my business—product and/or service?
_____
_____
_____
_____

2. How can I make my business, brand, and products better known in the marketplace through paid media or free publicity, word-of-mouth, or social media?

_____
_____
_____
_____

3. How can I move my customers down the Purchase Funnel?

_____
_____
_____
_____

4. What is my story to which people can relate? How can my story create awareness and publicity so people will buy my product/service?

_____
_____
_____
_____
_____
_____
_____

5. Who can help me sell my products and services? (e.g., family, friends, colleagues, collaborative relationships, etc.)

_____
_____
_____
_____

6. What are creative ways to promote my name, business name, product, and service?

_____
_____
_____
_____

Chapter 7. How to Select the Right Target Audience

"Getting a handle on what your customers really value is a critical part of becoming a good marketer." – Tom Patty (p. 101)

How to Define Your Target Audience

1. What does my target audience **do** that is relative to my product and service?
   Ex. What does Chiat/Day's target audience do? – They buy advertising.

   My target audience buys (action) _____
   _____

2. How often (frequency) or how much (quantity) does my target audience buy?
   Ex. The CEO or Marketing Manager has control of an advertising budget greater than $25 million.

   _____
   _____
   _____

3. What does my target audience **value**?
   Ex. The CEO or Marketing Manager who controls an advertising budget greater than $25 million, values breakthrough advertising.

   _____
   _____
   _____

Sometimes Your Clients Choose You

1. Have I ever experienced periods of my life when businesses or people chose me (desired to work with me)? How can I leverage these clients to expand my business?

   _____
   _____
   _____

Chapter 8. How to Use Your Best Customers to Grow Your Business

"You may have to direct your marketing to users, as well as your customers." – Tom Patty (p. 109)

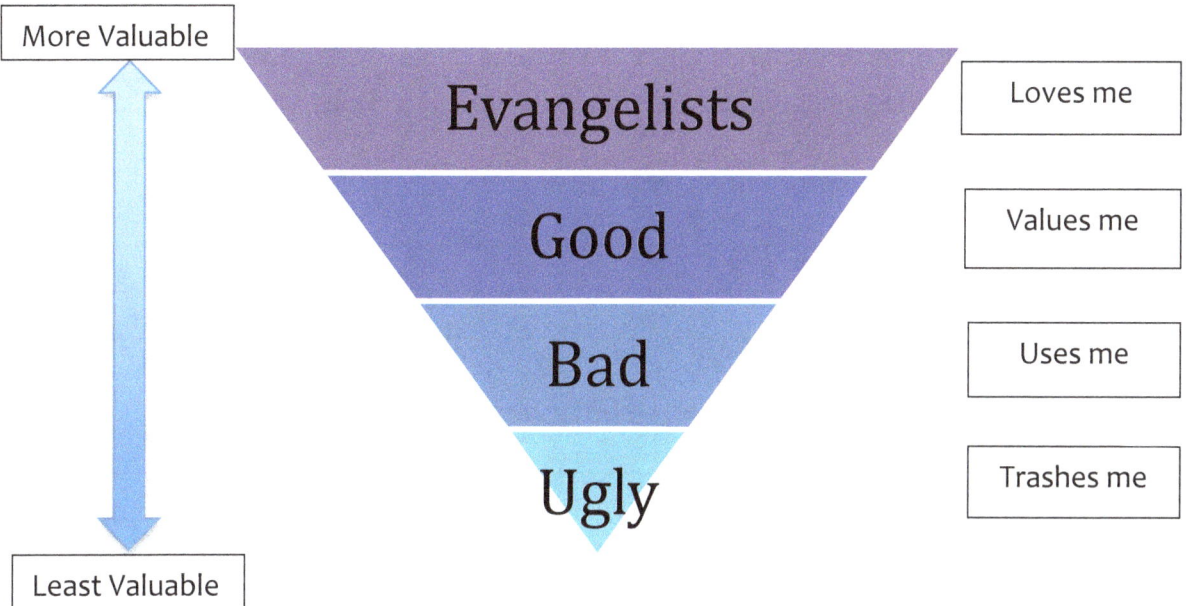

Customers	Customer Explanation	Your Customer Base
Evangelists	*"This is the ultimate, the perfect customer who raves about how great I am to everyone they know."* - Tom Patty (p. 111)	
Good	Content and consistently buys my product/service.	
Bad	Only buys my products/services when I have a deal. Bargain hunters.	
Ugly	Only buys my products/services when I have a deal. They pay late, complain and negative.	

1. How many customers/clients do I have?
   _____
   _____
   _____

2. How many good customers do I have?
   _____
   _____
   _____

3. What are the criteria for good customers?
   _____
   _____
   _____

4. How many people visit my store, website, bio, etc.?
   _____
   _____
   _____

5. What are some ways to attract good customers?
   _____
   _____
   _____

Chapter 9. How to Promote One Benefit

"Some people call this a mission statement or a vision. No matter what it's labeled, it comes down to understanding your agenda, your purpose, your "why!" – Tom Patty (p. 123)

Consumer's Point of View

"Your job as a smart marketer is to help prospective consumers figure out the critical benefits about your product or service as quickly and as easily as possible." – Tom Patty, (p 121)

1. What does this product/service do?

_____
_____
_____

2. How and when does it fit into my life?
___
___
___

3. How is it different/better than what already exists?
___
___
___

4. Why should I believe or trust this product/service?
___
___
___

5. What specific benefits are most important to my target (not everyone)?
___
___
___

[p. 122]

Brand/Products/Services	Benefit(s)
Chipotle	Fast/Easy

What Do You Stand for?

"It is difficult to promote one benefit if you do not know what your business or brand stands for." – Tom Patty (p. 123)

1. What does my business stand for?
   _____
   _____
   _____

2. What am I trying to do?
   _____
   _____
   _____

3. What is the purpose of my business?
   _____
   _____
   _____

4. Let's dig deeper. What is my business perspective? Am I just selling things or am I trying to solve my client's needs? Is it just for the money or something else? What is my WHY?
   _____
   _____
   _____
   _____
   _____
   _____

5. Review pages 124-125 in Tom's book. Where would I place my business? Place an X in the quadrant.

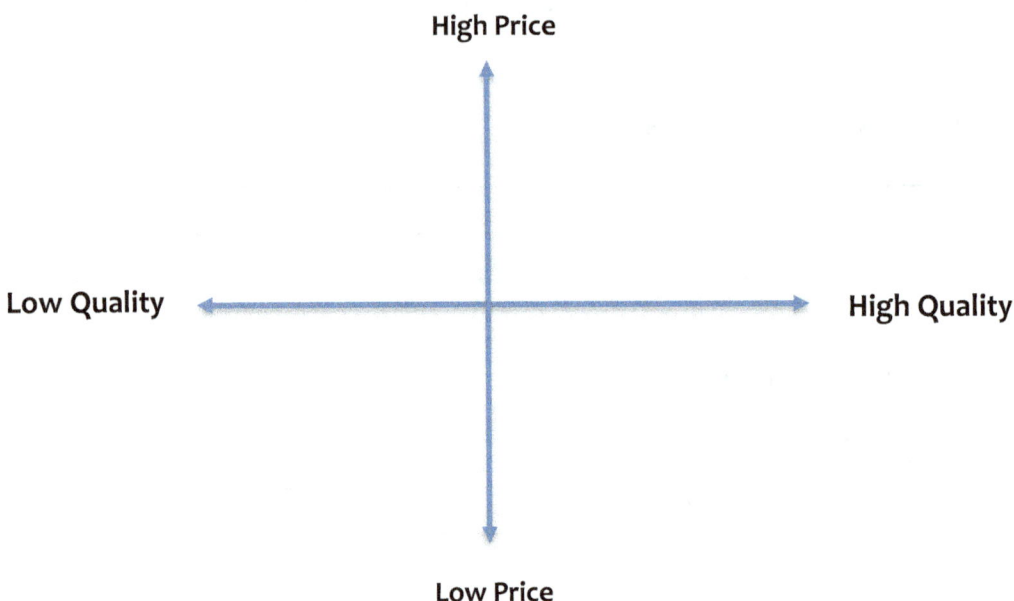

6. What am I Promoting?

7. What do I want to be known for?
_____
_____
_____
_____

8. What is the primary benefit I want to promote?
_____
_____
_____

Chapter 10. How to Improve Your Value Equation

". . . Focus on value. Price, in the end, means little." - Tom Patty (p. 133)

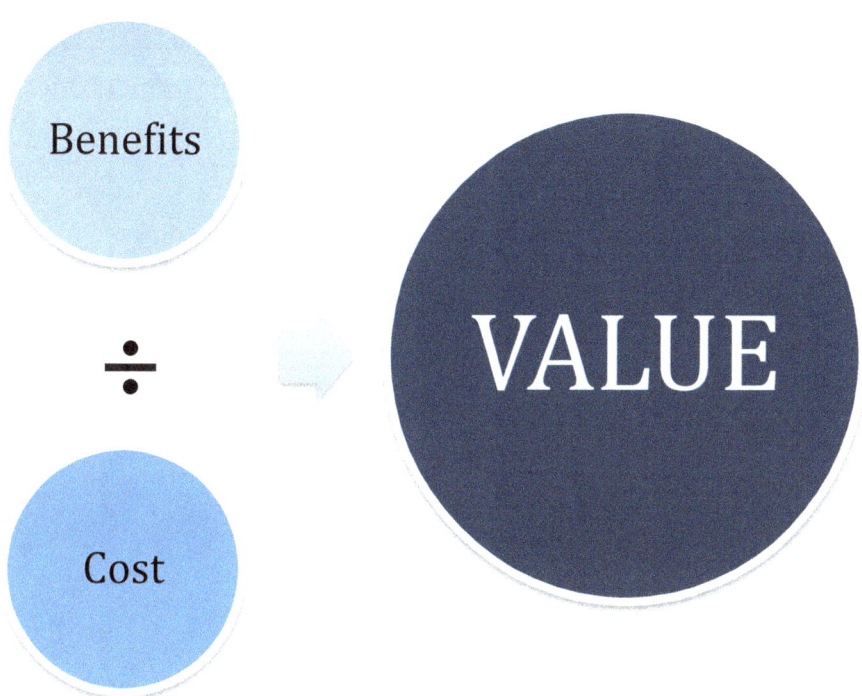

1. How important is the expense relative to the perceived value of benefits I will get from it?

_____
_____
_____

"To improve the value equation of your product or service, you must either increase the benefits or reduce the price." – Tom Patty (p. 134)

2. How important is the expense relative to the perceived value of benefits my customers will get from it?

_____
_____
_____

Chapter 11. How to Understand and Use the Purchase Funnel

"Not everyone NEEDS to be aware of your product or service, only those customers or clients who are likely to make a purchase."
– Tom Patty (p. 145)

What is the Purchase Funnel?
[p. 139-140]

Awareness
(Make sure people know about your business, product, or service)

Consider
(Provide new, relevant, & compelling information)

Shop
(Comparisons and possibly polarities)

Intend
(Almost but not yet...)

Buy
(Good but almost not finished)

Love

How Will I Move My Customers Down the Purchase Funnel?
[p. 140-154]

		Move My Customers down the Purchase Funnel			What will I do?
G O	**GO** where they are	Awareness	Who's my target audience? Find them and generate awareness.		
G	**GET** their attention	Awareness	What will engage their interest? Words? Display? Better headline?		
E	**ENGAGE** them by letting them sample or play for free	Demonstrate Consider	Will it solve a problem? What are the most compelling benefits of the product/service? Ambience?		
T	**TRADE** something for email	Reciprocity Consider	What will I provide?		
R	**ROUTE** them to landing page	Consider	What other options will the customer have? Competition? Time to convince!		
O	Create **OFFER** designed to get prospect to put something in shopping cart	Intention	What will I have to say or provide in order for the person to buy? (e.g. infomercials)		
I	Provide extra **INCENTIVE** to close deal NOW	Buy	Very close. What else do you need to do to close the deal? (free, more incentives, etc.)		
L O V E	Make it easy for the customer to let others know how much they **LOVE** your products or services	LOVE	I want them!		

Chapter 12. How to Use the Right Strategy to Grow Your Business

"Grow your business by exceeding the client's expectation!" –Tom Patty (p. 157)

Two Ways

1. Get more money from existing customers by exceeding my client's expectations
2. Get more new customers

Activity: Make a list of all of my clients. First, rank them by the amount of annual revenue I receive from each one. Then, base it on the potential they represent I can receive for more money.

Rank	Customer	Annual Revenue	Potential Revenue
		E.g. They set aside $10,000 in donations	E.g. They give me $1,000. I have the potential of receiving $9,000.

Product-Oriented Business

- Have customers buy products more frequently
- Communicate with existing customers frequently using various media platforms (e.g. email, phone, etc.)

My Product(s)	How Can I Increase the Frequency? What's My Strategy?

Service-Oriented Business

- Get satisfied customers to recommend my business, product or service
- Remind clients what I have done for them by giving the client the credit for their success (help clients shine)
- Have their testimonials/successes be publicized
- Know the various steps involved in the new business process

My Service(s)	How Can I Improve My Service-Oriented Business?

> *"Almost every client with an advertising/marketing budget of $25 million or more probably already has an advertising agency... be aware of what is going on with other clients and their relationships with their agencies. Is the client happy with the agency or disappointed?"* – Tom Patty (p. 165)

Typical 4 Stage Process to Acquire New Customers

- **Long List** (Invitation to Participate) – example is a Request for Proposal (RFP)

- **Short List** (Credentials Presentation) – Some credential checking questions would include how many employees? How many offices? What other clients? Case studies showing how my business has handled certain situations.

- **Final List** (Pitch) – Present winning presentations as to why companies should hire me. Remember, first impressions count.

- **Winner**

New Customer Acquisition	Conversion Ratio How many do I receive in a month/year?	How Can I Improve?
Invitation to Participate Request for Proposals		
Credentials Presentation		
Pitch Presentation		
Win the Proposal		
New Contracts with the Same Customer?		

Chapter 13. The Importance of You

> *". . . the single most important difference between success and failure is the leadership of the company, the person in charge."* – Tom Patty (p. 173)

Have the End in Mind

Let's go back to the Preface section and now answer these questions:

1. As the leader, how will I determine success, know where my destination is, and navigate to reach my destination?
   _____
   _____
   _____

2. What is my purpose? Is my purpose clear?
   _____
   _____
   _____

> *". . . one of the biggest single factors that separates successful business owners from the less successful is their clarity of purpose combined with a passionate intensity to make something better for consumers."*
> -Tom Patty (p. 174)

3. How is my purpose and passion aligned to creating products and services that will better humankind?
   _____
   _____
   _____

Chapter 14. Conclusion

"In business, if you successfully figure out how to serve the wants and needs of your targeted prospects and you do this better than your competition, you can make a lot of money."
– Tom Patty (p. 175)

Time to launch an impactful, results-oriented profitable business!

Biography Sarai Koo, Ph.D.

Executive Leader | Culture Change Engineer | Coach | Speaker | Author

www.saraikoo.com | www.projectSPICES.com

Most revered for her revolutionary, time-sensitive presentations, Dr. Sarai Koo has been developing people all over the world to live happier and healthier lives. She is a transformative speaker, culture change engineer, coach, author, and community leader.

Dr. Koo is a seasoned, award-winning executive with numerous years of leadership experience in human capital, talent development, organizational development, change management, human development/rights, training/instruction, cross-cultural/intercultural, and diversity and inclusion at for-profit and non-profit, local and Federal Government, Intelligence Communities, and global organizations.

Sarai is an expert at driving organizational change, developing leaders, and enhancing corporate culture to elevate employee engagement, improve skills and performance, and elevate overall results. She is a data-driven leader with high emotional intelligence competencies to manage multi-disciplinary teams and complex projects simultaneously to achieve company goals.

Dr. Koo is the CEO and Founder of Project SPICES, a coaching, consultancy and speaking firm. She creates programs and services for other companies and their leaders in leadership development, organizational behavior, DEI, and workforce transformation to advance new ways of doing things. She uses her SPICES Paradigm™, a process-oriented, decision-making approach to develop people to become productive; assist workforce personnel to explore their respective strengths, recognize and maintain positive relationships and work-life balance; become aware of and release hindering behavior, and design a life plan that fulfills their potential.

She appears on national and international media; coaches people globally; and speaks at various universities, companies, nonprofit organizations, non-governmental associations, schools, and governmental agencies (CIA, ODNI, State, etc.).

www.ingramcontent.com/pod-product-compliance
Lightning Source LLC
Chambersburg PA
CBHW060427010526
44118CB00017B/2397